Contents

D1584183

Published by: British Diabetic Association
British Diabetic Association ©
Photography: Bill Reavell
Front cover photograph: Pasta frttata page 27
Recipes developed by: Louise Tyler

Creative recipes for all occasions

Introduction

It isn't always easy to make sure that you and your family are eating healthy, balanced meals. You might be cooking in a hurry, only fancy a light meal, or be entertaining friends. Whatever situation you find yourself in, this British Diabetic Association cookbook aims to prove that there is a healthy recipe to fit the occasion. And we promise that you won't have to compromise on taste or style! To make the book as simple to use as possible, we've divided the recipes into the following sections:

Soups and starters

Soups and starters can be as filling or as light as you want. Use vegetables as a basis and serve with plenty of bread to make a light meal or snack - ideal for when you're short on time or when you don't fancy anything too substantial.

Light meals and lunches

Most days you will probably only have time for a quick lunch or light meal. These recipes are based on starchy carbohydrate foods like bread and potatoes and store cupboard ingredients such as eggs and tinned beans. Together they create simple and convenient meals.

Midweek meals

Midweek meals need to be quick and easy to prepare. Pasta, rice and other grains are ideal starchy foods to use as a basis for these meals. The recipes in this section provide you with a variety of new ideas to brighten up midweek food and provide balanced meals for you and your family.

Creative recipes for all occasions

Easy entertaining

Cooking a special meal for friends and family means going to a little extra trouble. These recipes use some of the more unusual ingredients and have a more extravagant taste despite being adapted to be lower in fat and salt. Just remember that when you are eating a special meal or entertaining guests, you can balance your menu choices. For instance, if you have a rich main course with pastry or a cream sauce, choose a light pudding like Jellied berry terrine on page 72. So don't feel guilty about indulging yourself when you are eating out or on a special occasion.

Delicious desserts

The recipes in this chapter show how even delicious puddings can still be low in fat. We should all be eating more fruit than we do, so we've devised some mouthwatering recipes which will help you do just this. Fruit provides an excellent basis for puddings. It is refreshing, nutritious, fat free and high in fibre and vitamins. If you have diabetes you can still choose puddings which contain sugar - as you will discover, it's possible to cut down on the amount of sugar without spoiling the taste.

Food Choice

Balanced eating is the key to everyday living with diabetes and to lifelong weight control. It isn't about restricting your food choice. Eating a wide variety of foods is essential to both the enjoyment of food and eating a healthy diet. Even high fat or high sugar foods can be included in your diet as long as the overall balance is right. Try not to think in terms of good or bad foods - to eat a healthy diet you just need to know how to achieve the right balance. The *Balance of Good Health*, shown on page 6 can help us all with this. It shows a variety of foods in the proportions we should be eating them.

Balanced meals

This cookbook, *Creative recipes for all occasions - balanced meals made easy*, is to help you and your family and friends to enjoy a wide variety of foods and recipes - some well balanced on their own but some need to be served with other foods like fruit, vegetables or bread which make them into balanced meals. We have provided serving suggestions which are intended to give you guidance on balancing your meals. One of the most important things you need to do is make sure the recipes are accompanied by starchy carbohydrate foods if they are not a good source on their own.

For instance you can enjoy a higher fat dish or a dish that might be higher than usual in sugar or salt if you eat it with foods that are low in fat, sugar or salt. A main course dish such as meat or fish pie made with a pastry case is higher in fat than a meat or fish casserole but this doesn't mean you can never have pie. Serve it with plenty of vegetables and a starchy carbohydrate food like potatoes to make the meal nutritionally well balanced. If you are having a pudding to follow, choose a fruit based recipe which is low in fat rather than a pie with more pastry.

You should still try to limit high fat, high sugar foods, especially if you are overweight, but balancing meals can help you to control your blood glucose levels and your weight more easily whilst still enjoying a wider range of foods.

About the recipes

The healthy diet for people with diabetes is the healthy diet for everyone - regardless of whether they have diabetes or not. Although people with diabetes do not need special recipes, our recipes have been devised to make them lower in fat, salt and sugar, and high in fibre but still deliciously appetising. Our tips will also help you to modify your own recipes. We have taken care to make the recipes quick and easy to prepare. Recipes which are particularly low in fat or high in fibre are highlighted by a colour code.

You can also use the nutrition information on food labels to compare foods and decide what you need to eat to balance your meals and snacks. We've provided the nutrition information for each recipe per serving.

This book also contains tips for making a recipe more substantial or suggestions for serving dishes as light meals. If you are following a vegetarian, gluten free or milk free diet we've included a special index to help you to identify suitable recipes at a glance (see page 78).

Balanced eating with diabetes

Following the principles of balanced eating benefits everyone. Making changes to your diet can also help you to manage your diabetes more easily, so this is something you need to think about. Changing your eating habits and your food choices can help to control blood glucose levels and blood fats and also to regulate weight. The amount of food that that you need to eat to control your weight will depend on your individual requirements. Therefore, the BDA recommends that people with diabetes should see a state registered dietitian for specific advice based on individual needs.

Here are some general guidelines which everyone can benefit from following:

● It is important to enjoy a wide variety of foods and to eat regular meals and snacks based on starchy carbohydrate foods like pasta, bread, rice, potatoes and cereals.

● Eat plenty of fruit, vegetables and pulses - aim for at least five portions a day to provide you with vitamins and fibre as well as helping to balance your overall diet.

● Cut down on fat, particularly saturated fat, and choose low fat dairy products such as skimmed milk (except for children under five years of age), lean meat, fish and poultry. Use less fat and salt in cooking and try not to add extra salt to food.

● Limit sugar, particularly sugary drinks, but remember that sugar is acceptable in baking and as an ingredient in foods like baked beans and tinned soups. Your meals do not have to be sugar free - sugar is fine as part of balanced eating.

Balance of good health

Foods can be divided into five main groups. In order for us to be enjoying a balanced diet we need to eat foods from all five of these groups in the right proportions.

Fruit and vegetables: it's easy to enjoy a wide variety whether fresh, frozen or canned. Aim to eat at least five servings a day.

Bread, cereals and potatoes base all meals and snacks on starchy foods from this group and choose high fibre varieties whenever you can.

Meat, fish and alternatives: choose lean meat and lower fat alternatives whenever you can.

Fatty and sugary foods: try not to eat these too often

Milk and Dairy Foods: choose lower fat alternatives on a regular basis.

*This illustration is based on the **Balance of Good Health**, published by the Department of Health, Ministry of Agriculture, Fisheries and Food and the Health Education Authority.*

- So-called 'diabetic' foods are not recommended. They still contain the same amount of fat and calories as standard foods. Diabetic foods contain alternative sweeteners to sugar such as sorbitol and isomalt. These types of sweeteners are known as nutritive or bulk sweeteners and they provide no special benefit to people with diabetes. Artificial sweeteners which are sugar and calorie free - like aspartame, acesulfame potassium or saccharin - can be used to sweeten drinks and sprinkle on stewed fruit or cereals if desired.

A question of carbohydrate

Starchy carbohydrates should form the basis of all meals - gone are the days when people with diabetes were advised to restrict these foods. Although different carbohydrate foods have different effects on blood glucose levels (see glycaemic index, below), all starchy foods provide you with energy, vitamins, minerals and fibre and are therefore an important part of healthy eating. Starchy foods are filling so eating plenty of them means you will tend to eat smaller portions of the protein foods like meat and fatty foods like cheese.

Some people with diabetes are advised to eat snacks between meals and at bedtime in order to spread carbohydrate intake more evenly over the day. This can help you to control blood glucose levels more easily. Snack foods can be high in fat and calories, so take care if you are trying to lose weight.

Glycaemic index

The glycaemic index (GI) is a ranking of individual foods according to the effect they have on blood glucose levels. Carbohydrate foods with a low GI cause a slow, steady rise in blood glucose levels. High GI foods cause blood glucose levels to rise quickly. This is because they are digested and absorbed more rapidly. For example, the GI of glucose is 100 whereas the GI of baked beans is 48. Even though you may not have heard the term GI before, you may already have been encouraged to include low GI foods such as pasta and pulses in your diet.

You can't tell a low GI food just by looking at it - and GI is not just related to the fibre or sugar content of a food. The effect of a meal or snack on blood glucose levels is influenced by many things. For example, the way in which a food is cooked and prepared, the combination of foods you eat with it and their fat and protein content, as well as other foods you have eaten that day, can all have a bearing on its GI.

There is more to eating a healthy diet than just eating low GI foods - a food is not good or bad because of its GI. It is neither necessary, nor practical to look at specific GI values for every food you eat. However, including more low GI foods in your meals can help to improve blood glucose control.

Low GI foods

Fruit: Eating apples, apricots, cherries, grapefruit, oranges, peaches, pears

Vegetables: sweet potato, sweetcorn, pulses (eg peas, chick peas, butter beans, kidney beans, baked beans, lentils)

Pasta

Wholegrains: barley, bulgar wheat, Basmati rice

Breakfast cereals such as porridge, All Bran, muesli

Milk, yogurt

Pumpernickel or rye bread, pitta bread, fruit loaf (heavy with fruit)

Plain popcorn

Oatmeal

Fibre

Most high fibre foods contain a combination of both soluble and insoluble fibre. Insoluble fibre used to be known as 'roughage'. This type of fibre is found in foods such as wheat cereals. It reduces the amount of time foods stay in the gut which helps to prevent problems such as constipation. Soluble fibre is found in oat bran, pulses (peas, beans and lentils) and fruit and vegetables. This type of fibre can be helpful in controlling blood glucose levels and reducing blood fats.

The average adult needs to eat about 18g of fibre a day. All our recipes have been coded high fibre if they contain 3g or more fibre per serving.

Wholemeal bread, wholewheat pasta and wholegrain cereals are higher fibre choices, but eating a high fibre diet does not have to mean eating wholemeal foods all the time. If you do choose a lower fibre starchy food, combine it during the meal with other higher fibre foods such as vegetables, pulses or fruit. For example, add dried fruit or a chopped banana to lower fibre breakfast cereal. If you want to have a white crusty roll which is lower in fibre choose a high fibre food like lentil or vegetable soup to go with it.

Creative recipes for all occasions

How to increase the fibre content of meals

Eat large servings of vegetables or salad

Add extra vegetables and pulses to soups and casseroles

Leave skins on potatoes

Add dried fruit to puddings, cereals, cakes, biscuits and even savoury dishes such as curries and salads

Add tinned pulses, rice or pasta to salads

Add peas, sweetcorn or cooked kidney beans to rice towards the end of cooking

Make fruit based puddings

Use some wholemeal flour as a substitute for white flour in recipes. But you don't have to use 100% wholemeal in recipes such as sponge cakes as it may give a dry and heavy result

Focus on fat

Everyone knows it's important to limit the amount of fats, oils and fatty foods you eat. Use an oil that is high in monounsaturated fats (mainly olive oil and rapeseed oil) or polyunsaturated fats (vegetable oils like sunflower, safflower, corn and soya oils). It's particularly important to eat less saturated animal fat. A diet high in this type of fat is linked to heart disease - and if you have diabetes you are already at greater risk of developing heart disease.

Being overweight makes diabetes more difficult to control so maintaining a healthy weight is an important part of treatment. Fat is the most concentrated source of calories. Cutting down on fat will help you to lose weight and help to prevent weight gain in the long term (most people tend to put on weight as they get older). Keeping active will also help to reduce your risk of developing heart disease and help you to control your weight.

As a guideline, an average man should aim to have no more than 95g of fat per day and an average woman 70g per day. Keep this guideline in mind and it will help you to assess whether a food is high in fat or not when looking at food labels - but remember to bear in mind the quantity of the food you intend to eat too, and the amount of fat you will be getting from other foods.

How to reduce the fat content of meals

Cut off any visible fat from meat and remove skin from poultry before cooking

Cook mince in a non-stick pan and drain off any excess fat before adding anything else to the pan.

Use skimmed milk and other low fat dairy products such as low fat yogurt in recipes. Use light crème fraîche in place of soured cream - it's heat stable and therefore ideal in savoury sauces. It's also delicious served on hot or cold puddings

Use low fat fromage fraîs in desserts or dips in place of cream or Greek yogurt where the recipe does not require cooking. If you prefer cream use single or whipping cream in place of double cream where possible

Don't add fat or oil when cooking unless you have to

Use a measuring spoon if following a recipe

Grill, poach, steam or microwave foods rather than cooking in oil or fat

Pastry is high in fat so use only one pastry crust when making pies

When using cheese in cooking use a small amount of strong cheese for all the flavour with less fat

Grate cheese - it goes further

Creative recipes for all occasions

Guide to recipe colour coding

Although all recipes have been devised to to be lower in fat, sugar, salt and higher in fibre, the colour coding highlights those recipes that are particularly high in fibre and low in fat.

 High fibre: 3g or more fibre per serving.

 Low fat: 5g or less fat per serving.

Polyunsaturated fats (sunflower, safflower, corn and soya oils) and monounsaturated fats (olive and rapeseed oils) are used instead of saturated fats (butter, lard) in the recipes.

kcal = kilocalorie
g = grams

 Denotes nutritional or cooking tips about the recipe.
Tips in red are particularly relevant to people with diabetes.

SOUPS
and starters

Noodle soup

low fat

This soup is low in fat and makes a low calorie starter using store cupboard ingredients. To make a light lunch, serve with wholemeal or granary bread for extra carbohydrate and fibre.

Serves: 2
Not suitable for freezing

600ml/1 pint good chicken or vegetable stock

100g/3¹/₂ oz dried egg noodles

4 spring onions, sliced

50g/1³/₄oz frozen peas

50g/1³/₄oz cooked prawns, defrosted if frozen

25g/1oz beansprouts

1 teaspoon soy sauce

Bring the chicken stock to the boil. Add the noodles and simmer for 4 minutes. Add the remaining ingredients 1 minute before the end of cooking time. Serve immediately.

This soup is also delicious using cooked chicken instead of prawns. To give the soup a bit of a kick add a few drops of chilli sauce.

Per serving:

Energy: 93kcal	Protein: 10g	Carbohydrate: 9g	Fat: 2g

Green bean soup ✓

High fibre

This soup contains dried and tinned pulses and is therefore high in soluble fibre and a good source of carbohydrate. It has a Mediterranean flavour because it contains pesto and herbs. It makes a delicious light meal served with Italian style bread.

Serves: 2
Not suitable for freezing

1 teaspoon olive oil
1 small leek, sliced
1 clove garlic, crushed
1 teaspoon fresh thyme, chopped
450ml/³/₄ pints vegetable stock
15g/¹/₂oz dried green lentils
25g/1oz French beans, halved
1 x 400g can flageolet beans, drained and rinsed
25g/1oz frozen peas
2 teaspoons green pesto
salt and freshly ground black pepper

Heat the oil in a medium saucepan, add the leek, garlic and thyme and fry for 3-4 minutes, until beginning to soften. Add the stock and lentils, bring to the boil, cover and simmer for 25 minutes or until the lentils are tender, adding the French beans, flageolets beans and peas 5 minutes before the end of cooking time. Season well. Transfer to serving dishes and top with a teaspoon of pesto.

 Stock cubes can be high in salt - look out for lower salt ones. Using herbs and spices in foods allows you to add less salt when cooking.

Per serving:

Energy: 148kcal	Protein: 8.4g	Carbohydrate: 16g	Fat: 5.6g

Smoked fish chowder

Low fat   *High fibre*

Potatoes form the basis of this soup making it a good source of carbohydrate. This recipe is low in fat and high in fibre and makes a filling starter or light meal on its own. Serve with extra bread for a more substantial meal.

Serves: 2
Suitable for freezing

Green bean soup

200g/7oz smoked haddock, skinned and cubed
300ml/¹/₂ pint skimmed milk
I small onion, chopped
250g/9oz floury potatoes, cubed
150ml/¹/₄ pint fish stock
50g/1³/₄ oz frozen sweetcorn
50g/1³/₄ oz frozen peas
2 tablespoons fresh parsley chopped
salt and freshly ground black pepper

Place the haddock in a saucepan, pour over the milk, place over a medium heat, bring to the boil, cover and simmer for 5-6 minutes or until the fish is cooked through. Remove the fish from the milk, flake and set aside. Add the onion and potato to the pan, bring to the boil, cover and simmer for 15-20 minutes or until the potatoes are cooked. Lightly mash half of the potato with the back of a fork. Add the remaining ingredients including the fish, to the pan and continue to cook for a further 5 minutes, then serve.

 As an alternative use haddock or cod in place of smoked fish.

Per serving:

Energy: 253kcal	Protein: 28g	Carbohydrate: 28g	Fat: 3.7g

Spiced parsnip and apple soup   Low fat   High fibre

Rich tasting but still low in fat, serve this spicy soup with naan bread.
Serves 4
Suitable for freezing

I teaspoon olive oil
450g/1lb parsnips, peeled and chopped
I onion, chopped
I teaspoon ground cumin
I teaspoon ground coriander
3 eating apples, peeled, cored and chopped
900ml/1¹/₂ pints good vegetable stock
4 tablespoons light crème fraîche
salt and freshly ground black pepper

Heat the oil in a medium non-stick frying pan. Add the parsnip and onion, fry for 3-4 minutes, add the cumin and coriander and continue to fry for one minute. Add the apples and stock, bring to the boil, cover and simmer for 15-20 minutes, until the parsnips are tender. Transfer to a food processor or blender and process until smooth. Return to the pan and stir through the crème fraîche, season well, heat through and serve.

 Light crème fraîche can be heated but it is lower in fat than single cream and has only a third of the fat of standard crème fraîche.

Per serving:

Energy: 158kcal	Protein: 3.5g	Carbohydrate: 25.3g	Fat: 5.4g

Spicy bean paté

Low fat High fibre

This recipe can be served with vegetable crudités as a low fat, low calorie starter or appetiser. For a light lunch or snack, serve with toast or crusty bread and salad.

Serves: 4
Suitable for freezing

1 teaspoon olive oil
1 onion, chopped
1 red chilli, finely chopped
1 clove garlic, crushed
1 teaspoon ground cumin
1 teaspoon ground coriander
1 teaspoon paprika
1 x 400g can red kidney beans
2 tomatoes, chopped
2 tablespoons fresh coriander, chopped

Heat the oil in a large non-stick frying pan. Add the onion, chilli and garlic and fry for 2-3 minutes or until softened. Remove the seeds from the chilli if you prefer a less fiery taste. Add the cumin, coriander and paprika and continue to cook for 1 minute. Stir through the beans and tomato and heat through. Transfer the mixture to a food processor or blender and blend until almost smooth, but still retaining a little texture. Stir through the coriander and serve.

Pulses such as beans and lentils have a low glycaemic index which means that eating them regulary will help to even out blood glucose levels.
Use different types of beans to suit what you have in your store cupboard eg butter beans or cannellini beans.

Per serving:

Energy: 98kcal	Protein: 6g	Carbohydrate: 16g	Fat: 5g

Toasts with pear and stilton

low fat

In this recipe, fruit, cheese and bread make a low calorie starter which is delicious served on salad leaves. You can make this dish into a light meal or lunch using three or four slices of bread per serving.
Serves: 4
Not suitable for freezing

4 thick slices French stick
1 x 60g pack prepared watercress
1 large ripe pear, cored and sliced
50g/1³/₄oz Stilton, sliced
salt and freshly ground black pepper

Preheat the grill and toast the bread on both sides. Cover the pieces of toast with the watercress, layer over the pear then top with the Stilton. Season then place under the grill for 1 minute or until the Stilton has begun to melt.
Serve immediately.

Topping variations:
For variety try topping toasted breads with other ingredients such as tomatoes, onions, parma ham, pastrami, crispy bacon, anchovies, ham, poached egg, or reduced fat cream cheese.

Bread is an ideal basis for snacks and starters. For extra fibre, use a wholemeal or granary French stick.

Per serving:

Energy: 119kcal	Protein: 49g	Carbohydrate: 14g	Fat: 5g

Creative recipes for all occasions

Toasts with pear and stilton

Aubergine dip

Low fat

This dip is low in calories. Serve with vegetable crudités or breadsticks. For a light lunch serve with plenty of warmed pitta bread to provide carbohydrate.

Serves: 6
Not suitable for freezing

2 medium aubergines, halved lengthways
2 teaspoons olive oil
1 teaspoon ground coriander seeds, crushed
1 tablespoon sesame seeds
1 teaspoon paprika
2 cloves garlic, crushed
½ cm/¼ inch fresh ginger, peeled and grated
15g/½oz creamed coconut
2 tablespoons fresh coriander, chopped
salt and freshly ground black pepper

Preheat the oven to 200°C/400°F/gas mark 6.
Place the aubergines on a baking sheet, brush with half of the oil and bake for 40-45 minutes or until soft. Meanwhile, heat the remaining oil in a frying pan, add the coriander seeds, sesame seeds, paprika, garlic and ginger and fry for 2 minutes. Remove from the heat add the coconut and stir until melted. Remove the aubergine from the oven and scrape the flesh into a bowl and mash with a fork. Mix in the onion mixture and coriander. Combine well, season and serve.

Vegetables like aubergines can absorb a lot of oil when fried. Brushing them with a little oil and then baking can help to reduce overall fat content.

Per serving:

Energy: 75kcal	Protein: 1.8g	Carbohydrate: 2.7g	Fat: 2.5g

Mediterranean soft cheese dip

This dip makes a low calorie starter served with vegetable and fruit crudités or breadsticks. The dip contains no carbohydrate, so for a light meal, serve with potato wedges or bread.

Serves: 6
Not suitable for freezing

50g/1³/₄oz pitted black olives

2 tablespoons sun-dried tomato paste

handful fresh basil leaves

2 anchovy fillets

200g/7oz reduced fat soft cheese

salt and freshly ground black pepper

Place the olives, sun-dried tomato paste, basil and anchovies in a blender or food processor and process until almost smooth. Combine with the soft cheese and season well.

Reduced fat soft cheese can be used as a basis for patés, dips and sauces. Adding a little to soups gives a creaminess without too much extra fat.

Per serving:

Energy: 75kcal   Protein: 3.4g   Carbohydrate: 0g   Fat: 6.4g

Grilled sardines

Fish is a protein food and contains no carbohydrate or fibre. For a light lunch, serve with a salad such as tabbouleh and crusty bread.

Serves 4

Not suitable for freezing

8 fresh sardines, gutted and cleaned

grated rind and juice of 1 lemon

2 cloves garlic, crushed

3 tablespoons fresh parsley, chopped

1 tablespoon olive oil

salt and freshly ground black pepper

Place the sardines into a shallow non-metallic dish. Mix the remaining ingredients together, and pour over the sardines. Leave to marinate for at least one hour. Place the sardines under a pre-heated grill and cook for 7-8 minutes, turning occasionally until cooked through. Serve. This is ideal cooked on the barbecue in the summer.

The type of oil in oily fish (Omega 3) may be protective against heart disease. Aim to eat oily fish at least once a week.

Per serving:

Energy: 297kcal   Protein: 33.8g   Carbohydrate: 0g   Fat: 17.8g

and lunches

Warm bean salad

A well balanced dish on its own, but can also be served with crusty bread and extra salad leaves.

Serves: 2

Not suitable for freezing

2 tablespoons white wine vinegar
1 tablespoon olive oil
1 clove garlic, crushed
1 small onion, sliced
1 x 400g can butter beans or cannellini beans, drained and rinsed
2 tomatoes, chopped
½ cucumber, chopped
2 tablespoons fresh parsley, chopped
salt and freshly ground black pepper

Heat the vinegar and oil together in a pan and add the garlic, onion and beans, cover and simmer gently for 5-6 minutes. Stir through the tomato, cucumber and parsley, season and serve immediately.

Beans and pulses provide an excellent low fat source of protein and iron for vegetarians. Having some food or drink rich in vitamin C (such as fruit juice) with your meal will improve the absorption of iron.

Per serving:

Energy: 193kcal	Protein: 9.9g	Carbohydrate: 25g	Fat: 6.5g

Creative recipes for all occasions

Warm bean salad

Potato pancakes with poached egg

This recipe is ideal as a quick lunch or supper. Serve with vegetables to increase the fibre content of the meal - or alternatively follow with some fruit.

Serves: 1
Not suitable for freezing

225g/8oz floury potatoes, peeled and cubed
1 medium egg, beaten
2 tablespoons skimmed milk
2 teaspoons self-raising flour
2 teaspoons fresh oregano, chopped
1 large egg white, whisked until it forms soft peaks
1 teaspoon oil
1 medium egg
salt and freshly ground black pepper

Cook the potatoes in boiling water for 12-15 minutes or until cooked. Drain and mash until smooth. Stir in the beaten egg, milk, flour and oregano, season well then gently fold in the egg white.

Heat the oil in a non-stick frying pan, place spoonfuls of mixture into the pan and cook for 1-2 minutes on each side or until golden.

Meanwhile, bring a large pan of salted water to the boil, reduce the heat to give a very gentle simmer. Break the eggs into the water one at a time, gently stirring the water so the white wraps around the yolk. Remove from the heat and leave to poach in the water for three minutes. Remove with a slotted spoon then serve on the potato pancakes.

 Eggs provide a good cheap source of protein.

Per serving:

Energy: 520kcal	Protein: 15.8g	Carbohydrate: 23.1g	Fat: 12.8g

The young, the elderly, pregnant women and those suffering from immune-deficiency diseases should not eat raw or lightly cooked eggs to avoid the risk of salmonella.

Creative recipes for all occasions

Colcannon

High fibre

To make a complete meal serve with a low fat, high carbohydrate source of protein - baked beans are ideal.

Serves: 4
Not suitable for freezing

450g/1lb potatoes, peeled and chopped
450g/1lb savoy cabbage, sliced
1 teaspoon oil
4 spring onions, sliced
25g/1oz low fat spread
150ml/¼ pint skimmed milk
pinch of ground nutmeg
50g/1¾oz mature Cheddar, grated
salt and freshly ground black pepper

Boil the potatoes in a large pan of water until tender. Drain then mash until light and fluffy. Blanch the cabbage for 2-3 minutes then drain well. Heat the oil in a large pan and fry the spring onions until softened. Add the cabbage and continue to cook for 3-4 minutes. Stir in the potatoes, remaining low fat spread, milk and nutmeg then season well. Sprinkle over the cheese and place under a hot grill until golden and bubbling.

 Use skimmed milk in cooking to reduce the fat content.

Per serving:

Energy: 271kcal	Protein: 10g	Carbohydrate: 27g	Fat: 12.5g

Filo tartlets

Low fat

These tartlets are quite small but very tasty. To make a balanced meal serve with extra carbohydrate, such as bread or rice salad and plenty of salad leaves.

Serves: 4
Not suitable for freezing

4 sheets filo pastry (25cm/10 inch square)

1 tablespoon milk

8 cherry tomatoes, halved

100g/3½oz firm goat's cheese, cut into 4 slices

12 pitted black olives

2 teaspoons fresh oregano chopped

salt and freshly ground black pepper

Preheat the oven to 200°C/400°F/gas mark 6.

Brush each piece of filo with a little milk, then cut into quarters. Line 4 (8cm/3inch) loose-bottomed flan tins each with 4 squares of the pastry, then brush with any remaining milk. Place half of the tomatoes in the bottom of the tarts, cover with the cheese then top with the remaining tomatoes and the olives. Sprinkle over the oregano and season well. Cook for 10-15 minutes or until the pastry is golden and the cheese has begun to melt. Serve immediately.

If you prefer you could use Camembert or Brie instead of the goat's cheese. Although all pastry is high in fat, using filo allows you to use a lot less as a little goes a long way.

Per serving:

Energy: 89kcal Protein: 5g Carbohydrate: 6g Fat: 5g

Dahl

High fibre

Serve with Indian bread such as naan or chappatis, or with basmati rice and chutneys.

Serves: 4

Not suitable for freezing

225g/8oz yellow lentils, rinsed and drained (removing any little stones)

1 teaspoon turmeric

2 tablespoons vegetable oil

1 teaspoon cumin seeds

1 medium onion, chopped

2 cloves garlic, crushed

1 teaspoon cayenne pepper

2 tablespoons fresh coriander, chopped

Place the lentils and turmeric in a medium pan and pour over 750ml 1¼ pints of cold water. Bring to the boil, cover and simmer for 25-30 minutes or until tender.

Creative recipes for all occasions

Meanwhile, heat the oil in a frying pan and add the cumin, onion, garlic and cayenne pepper. Fry for 8 - 10 minutes or until the onion becomes a nutty brown colour, but not burnt. When the lentils have absorbed all the water, remove from the heat and beat with a wooden spoon until soft. Stir through the onion mixture and coriander. Serve immediately.

 Dahl is traditionally made using ghee, a type of clarified butter. This recipe uses less fat and an oil which is low in saturates.

Per serving:

Energy: 229kcal	Protein: 13.6g	Carbohydrate: 33g	Fat: 5.8g

Pasta frittata

This recipe should be served with new potatoes or bread for more carbohydrate. Add extra salad or vegetables for fibre.
Serves: 4
Not suitable for freezing

I teaspoon olive oil
2 rashers lean, smoked back bacon, chopped
I small red onion, sliced
I yellow pepper, deseeded and chopped
50g/1³/₄ oz cooked pasta shapes eg macaroni
75g/2³/₄ oz fresh baby spinach
3 medium eggs
I tablespoon fresh Parmesan, grated
I teaspoon fresh oregano, chopped
salt and freshly ground black pepper

Heat the oil in a small frying pan. Add the bacon, onion and pepper and fry for 2-3 minutes until the onion begins to soften. Stir in the pasta and spinach and continue to cook for I minute. Beat together the eggs, Parmesan and oregano. Season well then pour into the pan. Cook over a medium heat for 2-3 minutes, until beginning to set, then place the pan under a preheated grill for 2 minutes until golden and firm to touch. Serve immediately.

 Although Parmesan cheese is relatively high in fat its strong flavour means you only need to use a small amount.

Per serving:

Energy: 124kcal	Protein: 9.1g	Carbohydrate: 5g	Fat: 7.7g

Falafel with yogurt sauce

Being based on chickpeas, this recipe is high in fibre and packed with carbohydrate. Squeeze some salad leaves into the pittas along with the falafel, if you can find room.

Serves: 4
Suitable for freezing

1 x 400g can chickpeas, drained and rinsed
3 cloves garlic, crushed
1 teaspoon ground coriander
1 teaspoon ground cumin
1 small onion, chopped
1 tablespoon plain flour
2 tablespoons fresh coriander, chopped
2 teaspoons oil
salt and freshly ground black pepper

Yogurt Sauce:

150g low fat natural yogurt
2 tablespoons fresh mint, chopped
2 tablespoons fresh coriander, chopped

To serve:

4 pitta bread
salad leaves

Place the chickpeas in a blender or a food processor with the garlic, spices and onion and blend until smooth. Spoon into a bowl, add the flour and coriander season well and stir until thoroughly combined. Form into 8 patties, brush with a little oil and cook under a preheated grill for 3-4 minutes on each side until golden and crisp. Meanwhile make the dip by mixing together all the in gredients. Serve in the pitta breads, with the sauce.

Traditionally this dish is deep fried. Brushing with oil and grilling reduces the fat content. Try this with other foods that you normally fry such as potato wedges.

Per serving:

Energy: 378kcal	Protein: 19g	Carbohydrate: 52g	Fat: 12g

Creative recipes for all occasions

Falafel with yogurt sauce

Sweet potato fishcakes

High fibre

This recipe has an oriental flavour. It is a good source of carbohydrate on its own. Serve with plenty of stir-fried vegetables, such as mangetout and baby sweetcorn.

Serves: 4
Not suitable for freezing

350g/12oz sweet potato, peeled and cut into chunks
350g/12oz potato, peeled and cut into chunks
2 x 170g cans crab, drained
2 tablespoons fresh coriander, chopped
1 red chilli, deseeded and finely chopped
3 spring onions, sliced
1 tablespoon lemon juice
1 teaspoon sesame oil
4 tablespoons sesame seeds
salt and freshly ground black pepper

For the dipping sauce:
2 tablespoons chilli sauce
2 tablespoons runny honey
2 tablespoons fresh coriander, chopped

Preheat the oven to 200°C/400°F/gas mark 6.
Place the sweet potato and ordinary potato into a pan of boiling water and simmer for 10-15 minutes or until tender. Drain, return to the pan and mash until smooth. Stir in the crab, coriander, chilli, spring onions and lemon juice. Form the mixture into patties, brush with a little oil then press into the sesame seeds.

Place the patties onto a baking sheet and bake for 10-12 minutes until golden and piping hot. Meanwhile, combine all the ingredients for the dipping sauce, then serve with the fishcakes.

Choosing orange fleshed sweet potatoes will provide you with a richer source of Vitamin A - a natural antioxidant. Antioxidants help protect against heart disease and cancer.

Per serving:

Energy: 290kcal	Protein: 15.9g	Carbohydrate: 40g	Fat: 8.5g

Creative recipes for all occasions

Warm pasta tuna niçoise

This salad is based on pasta, which is slowly absorbed and an excellent source of carbohydrate for people with diabetes. It makes a good balanced meal.

Serves: 4
Not suitable for freezing

350g/12oz dried pasta shapes
100g/3½ oz French beans, halved
1 tablespoon olive oil
4 x 125g/4½oz pieces fresh tuna steak
4 plum tomatoes, quartered
¼ cucumber, chopped
2 tablespoons capers, drained
2 hard boiled eggs, peeled and quartered
juice of 1 lemon
1 teaspoon Dijon mustard
pinch of sugar
fresh basil to garnish
salt and freshly ground black pepper

Cook the pasta according to the pack instructions, adding the beans 5 minutes before the end of cooking time. Drain. Meanwhile, brush the tuna steaks with a little oil and cook under a preheated grill for 3-4 minutes on each side. If fresh tuna is not available then use tuna tinned in water. Toss together the pasta, beans, tomatoes, cucumber, capers and egg in a large bowl. Mix together the remaining oil, lemon juice, mustard and sugar. Season well then stir through the pasta.

Divide between four dishes, top each with a piece of tuna and garnish with basil.

 Eggs contain cholesterol. However, blood cholesterol is more influenced by the total amount of saturated fat in the diet rather than the cholesterol in foods.

Per serving:

Energy: 565kcal	Protein: 44.4g	Carbohydrate: 67g	Fat: 14g

Hot chicken salad

For extra carbohydrate and fibre, serve with wholemeal or granary bread or a scone from page 33

Serves 2
Not suitable for freezing

1 teaspoon oil
1 large, boneless, skinless chicken breast, sliced
150g/5¹/₂oz new potatoes, cooked and halved
2 teaspoons wholegrain mustard
1 orange, segmented
juice of an orange
2 spring onions, sliced
1x 60g bag mixed lettuce leaves
2 tomatoes, chopped
salt and freshly ground black pepper

Heat the oil in a non-stick frying pan. Add the chicken and fry for 3-4 minutes until browned. Add the potatoes, mustard, orange and orange juice, stir and continue to cook for 1 minute. Toss together the spring onions, salad leaves and tomatoes. Divide between 2 plates, spoon over the chicken mixture and serve immediately.

 Save 5g of fat per portion by removing the skin from the chicken before cooking.

Per serving:

Energy: 269kcal	Protein: 32.1g	Carbohydrate: 15g	Fat: 8.9g

Herby pork burgers

Compared to traditional 'burgers' this recipe is lower in fat. You can use turkey mince instead of pork. Sandwich the burgers between a soft bap or burger roll and serve with salad and relish.

Serves: 4
Suitable for freezing

450g/1lb lean pork mince

3 tablespoons sage and onion stuffing mix,
mixed with 6 tablespoons boiling water

100g/3 ¹/₂oz ready-to-eat dried apricots, chopped

2 tablespoons tomato purée

1 small onion, finely chopped

2 teaspoons oil

salt and freshly ground black pepper

Preheat the grill to high.
Mix together all the ingredients except the oil in a large bowl and season well.
Shape the mixture into eight patties. Brush each side of the burger with a little
oil, place on a baking sheet and grill for 3-4 minutes on each side until cooked
through or alternatively barbecue. Serve immediately.

*Lean minced pork contains less than half the amount of fat as lean minced
beef.*

Per serving:

Energy: 209kcal   Protein: 26.3g   Carbohydrate: 12.6g   Fat: 6.3g

Bacon, sun dried tomato and rosemary scones

Although not a meal on their own, these sweet or savoury scones make ideal
snacks, or to accompany a light meal. They also make a tasty change to bread for
packed lunches or picnics.

Serves 4

Suitable for freezing

100g/3¹/₂oz self-raising flour

25g/1oz polyunsaturated margarine

2 pieces smoked, lean back bacon, grilled and chopped

2 sun-dried tomatoes in oil, chopped

1 tablespoon fresh rosemary, chopped

4 tablespoons milk

Pre-heat the oven to 220°C/425°F/gas mark 7.

Sift the flour into a large bowl and rub in the margarine until the mixture resembles fine breadcrumbs. Stir in the bacon, sun-dried tomatoes and rosemary. Gradually stir in enough milk to combine the ingredients. Place the dough on a lightly floured surface and press into a round approximately 2.5cm/1 inch thick. Using the back of a knife, mark into quarters. Place on a baking sheet. Brush with a little milk, then bake for 15-20 minutes until golden.

Per serving:

Energy: 162kcal	Protein: 4g	Carbohydrate: 20g	Fat: 8g

Variations:

Apple and cheese
Replace the bacon, sun-dried tomatoes and rosemary with one eating apple, peeled, cored and grated and 50g/1³/₄oz mature cheddar cheese, grated.

Banana and sunflower seed
Replace the bacon, sun-dried tomato and rosemary with one roughly mashed banana and 25g/1oz sunflower seeds.

Apricot and orange
Replace the milk with 4 tablespoons soured cream and the bacon, sun-dried tomato and rosemary with 50g/1³/₄oz chopped ready-to-eat dried apricots and the grated rind of 1 large orange. Add a little milk if the mixture is too dry.

Soufflé jacket potato

There is nothing easier than a jacket potato! Serve with plenty of salad.
Serves 2
Not suitable for freezing

2 large baking potatoes
1 teaspoon butter
2 tablespoons semi-skimmed milk
1 medium egg, separated
2 spring onions, sliced
25g/1oz lean ham, chopped
1 tablespoon chives, chopped
salt and freshly ground black pepper

Creative recipes for all occasions

Pre-heat the oven to 200°C/400°F/gas mark 6.

Prick the potatoes with a fork and cook in the oven for 1-1½ hours or until cooked through. Alternatively cook in a microwave. Remove from the oven and cut off a 1cm/½ inch slice lengthways and discard.

Scoop out the flesh from the potatoes and mash with the butter and milk until very smooth. Stir in the egg yolk, spring onions, ham and chives and season well. In a separate bowl whisk the egg white until stiff. Gently fold the egg white through the potato mixture then spoon into potato skins. Place on a baking sheet and return to the oven for 10-15 minutes until golden. Serve immediately.

Per serving:

Energy: 190kcal	Protein: 7.5g	Carbohydrate: 30g	Fat: 5.5g

Jacket potato and sandwich ideas

Nothing could be simpler when time is short than a sandwich or a jacket potato. If you are a little tired of the same old filling then try some of these ideas.

These recipes give enough to fill one jacket potato or a round of sandwiches. Adjust the size of potato or the amount of bread according to your appetite.

● Mix together, 25g/1oz reduced fat cream cheese, 1 tablespoon sultanas, 1 chopped stick celery, ½ chopped red pepper and 1 sliced spring onion. Season well.

● Mix together 100g/3½ oz frozen prawns (defrosted if frozen), 1 tablespoon fat free mayonnaise, 1 tablespoon chopped fresh parsley, and a few drops of tabasco.

● Mix together 50g/1¾oz cooked chicken breast, 1 chopped tomato, 1 tablespoon chopped fresh coriander, a little lime juice and 1 tablespoon reduced calorie coleslaw. Season well.

● Combine 1 tablespoon reduced fat cream cheese, 1 teaspoon pesto, 4 chopped black olives, 1 chopped tomato. Season well.

● Mix together 1 small grated carrot, 1 tablespoon lemon juice and 1 teaspoon wholegrain mustard then stir through 15g/½oz crumbled feta.

meals

Roasted vegetable pasta

High fibre

Pasta and vegetables are the basis of this recipe which makes a high carbohydrate, high fibre meal. For a non-vegetarian option stir through a little sliced lean ham or parma ham. Resist adding any extra cheese when serving as this will add to the calories.

Serves: 4

Not suitable for freezing

350g/12oz dried pasta shapes
1 courgette, sliced
1 red onion, cut into wedges
1 small aubergine, sliced
1 red pepper, sliced
1 yellow pepper, sliced
1 teaspoon olive oil
1 tablespoon fresh oregano, chopped
1 x 500ml jar passatta (sieved tomatoes)
4 tablespoons reduced fat cream cheese
15g/½oz pine nuts, toasted
salt and freshly ground black pepper

Cook the pasta according to the pack instructions. Meanwhile, place the vegetables onto a foil covered grill pan. Brush with the oil, sprinkle with the oregano and place under a preheated grill for 8-10 minutes. Turn occasionally until cooked and beginning to char in places. Heat the passatta in a pan and stir through the cream cheese until combined. Season well. Toss together the pasta, vegetables and passatta mixture. Divide between four plates and serve sprinkled with the toasted pine nuts.

Vegetables, like fruit, are naturally low in fat and calories. Eat more fruit and veg and don't be tempted to use a lot of oil when cooking them.

Per serving:

Energy: 433kcal	Protein: 14.4g	Carbohydrate: 80g	Fat: 8.2g

Creative recipes for all occasions

Golden topped gnocchi

High fibre

This Italian-style dish is high in fibre and is well balanced. It is also delicious served with a side salad or some fresh sliced plum tomatoes.
Serves: 4
Not suitable for freezing

For the gnocchi:
750g/1 ½ lb floury potatoes, peeled and cut into chunks
175g/6oz plain flour
2 medium egg yolks, beaten
salt and freshly ground black pepper

For the tomato sauce:
1 x 500g jar passata
1 clove garlic, crushed
2 tablespoons mixed fresh herbs, chopped

For the topping:
50g/1 ½oz fresh granary breadcrumbs
50g/1 ½oz fresh Parmesan, grated

Preheat the oven to 200°C/400°F/gas mark 6.
Cook the potatoes in boiling water until tender. Drain well then mash until quite smooth. Beat in all but 1 tablespoon of the flour and both egg yolks. Season well. Turn out onto a floured surface and knead, adding more flour if necessary to give a firm mixture. Roll walnut sized pieces of the dough into small sausage shapes and press with the back of a fork. Bring a large pan of water to a gentle simmer. Drop the gnocchi into the boiling water and cook in batches for 4-5 minutes until the gnocchi rise to the surface. Remove from the pan using a slotted spoon and place in an ovenproof dish.

Meanwhile, place all the ingredients for the tomato sauce into a pan, bring to the boil and simmer for 5 minutes. Pour the sauce over the gnocchi, mix together the breadcrumbs and Parmesan and sprinkle over the top. Place in the oven and cook for 10-12 minutes, or until the topping is golden. Serve immediately.

To make this delicious dish in moments, why not use ready made gnocchi which are available from supermarkets.

Per serving:

Energy: 442kcal	Protein: 15.8g	Carbohydrate: 81g	Fat: 8.4g

Red pepper, lentils and bulgar wheat

This dish is a complete vegetarian meal on its own. Serve with salad and bread to fill up.

Serves: 4

Not suitable for freezing

125g/4¹/₂oz dried puy or green lentils
1 teaspoon olive oil
1 onion, chopped
1 glove garlic, crushed
1 teaspoon ground cinnamon
900ml/1¹/₂pints vegetable stock
125g/4¹/₂oz bulgar wheat, toasted
100g/3¹/₂oz ready-to-eat dried apricots
2 red peppers, deseeded and quartered
75g/2³/₄oz Gruyère, cubed
2 tablespoons fresh mint, chopped

Place the lentils in a medium pan and add enough water to cover them by about 2.5cm/1inch. Bring to the boil and cook rapidly for 10 minutes, then drain and rinse under cold water. Heat the oil in a separate pan. Add the onion, garlic and ground cinnamon and fry for 3-4 minutes or until the onions are beginning to soften. Stir the lentils into the onion mixture. Add the stock and bulgar wheat. Bring to the boil, cover and simmer for 30 minutes or until the lentils are tender. Add the apricots 5 minutes before the end of cooking time. Remove the lid 10 minutes before the end of cooking time if there is a lot of excess liquid.

Meanwhile, place the peppers under a preheated grill and cook for 6-7 minutes, or until the skins are blackened, carefully remove the skins then slice the pepper into strips. Stir the red peppers and Gruyère into the bulgar mixture and season well. Serve immediately.

To toast bulgar wheat, place in a pan over a medium heat and cook for 2-3 minutes or until the grains begin to colour. Toasting gives the bulgar a deliciously nutty flavour when cooked.

Per serving:

Energy: 357kcal	Protein: 17.8g	Carbohydrate: 52g	Fat: 9.5g

Creative recipes for all occasions

Red pepper, lentils and bulgar wheat

Spinach and mushroom lasagne

High fibre

This is a higher fat dish so be sure to serve with a low fat accompaniment such as salad or peas.

Serves: 4
Suitable for freezing

1 teaspoon oil
1 onion, chopped
1 clove garlic, crushed
250g/8oz mushrooms, sliced
2 large carrots, peeled and grated
1 teaspoon mixed dried herbs
450g/1lb frozen spinach
1 x 200g carton light crème fraîche
9 sheets no-precook lasagne
1 x 150g carton low fat yogurt
1 medium egg, beaten
40g/1½oz mature cheddar, grated

Preheat the oven to 200°C/400°F/gas mark 6.

Heat the oil in a large pan. Add the onion, garlic and mushrooms and fry for 4-5 minutes until softened. Stir in the carrots, herbs and spinach and continue to fry for 5 minutes until the spinach has defrosted and most of the liquid has evaporated. Stir in the crème fraîche. Season well and remove from the heat. Spoon one third of the spinach mixture into the bottom of an ovenproof dish, cover with 3 sheets of lasagne then continue to layer up finishing with a layer of pasta. Beat together the yogurt and the egg and spoon over the lasagne. Sprinkle over the cheese and cook for 30-40 minutes or until the pasta is tender and the topping is golden.

Mixing together yogurt and egg is a quick and easy alternative to making a cheese sauce which can be flavoured as required.

Per serving:

Energy: 400kcal	Protein: 18.9g	Carbohydrate: 47g	Fat: 16.4g

Spicy crab tortilla

Although this recipe serves four, use enough tortillas to satisfy the appetites of the people eating. Serve this with shredded lettuce, chopped tomato and a little sliced avocado.

Serves: 4
Not suitable for freezing

1 teaspoon olive oil
1 onion, finely chopped
2.5cm/1inch fresh ginger, peeled and grated
1 clove garlic, crushed
1 teaspoon dried red chilli flakes
1 teaspoon ground cumin
2 x 170g can crab, drained
2 tablespoons fresh coriander, chopped
1 pack small flour tortillas

Heat the oil in a non-stick frying pan. Add the onion, ginger, garlic, chilli flakes and cumin and fry for 2-3 minutes. Remove the pan from the heat and stir in the crab and coriander. Warm the tortillas according to the pack instructions. Use the crab to fill the tortilla.

Tortillas are an alternative way of providing starchy carbohydrate with a meal.

Per serving:

Energy: 195kcal	Protein: 14.7g	Carbohydrate: 31g	Fat: 2.1g

Smoked fish florentine

This fish dish contains little carbohydrate so serve with rice or new potatoes and contrasting vegetables such as baby sweetcorn.

Serves: 3
Not suitable for freezing

15g/1/2oz plain flour

300ml/1/2pint skimmed milk

25g/1oz mature cheddar, grated

pinch nutmeg

1 clove garlic, crushed

1 x 225g bag fresh baby spinach leaves, rinsed

3 tomatoes, sliced

3 x 100g/3 1/2oz pieces smoked haddock

salt and freshly ground black pepper

Preheat the oven to 200°C/400°F/gas mark 6.

Make the cheese sauce by tipping the flour into a medium saucepan and gradually stir in the milk. Place over a medium heat, stirring continuously until thickened. Stir through half the cheese and the nutmeg and season well.

Meanwhile, place the garlic and spinach into a large pan, place over a medium heat and cook for 1-2 minutes or until the spinach has wilted and any moisture has evaporated.

Layer the tomatoes in the bottom of an ovenproof dish, spoon over the spinach, top with the haddock, and pour over the cheese sauce. Sprinkle over the remaining cheese and bake in the oven for 25-30 minutes, until golden and bubbling. Serve immediately.

 Fat is usually mixed with flour to form the basis of a white sauce. Our fat free method can be used to adapt other recipes.

Per serving:

Energy: 200kcal   Protein: 27.8g   Carbohydrate: 12.3g   Fat: 4.8g

Creative recipes for all occasions

Garlic and herb stuffed chicken

This simple homemade version of a family favourite, similar to chicken kiev, contains one third of the amount of fat as a ready prepared version. Serve with boiled new potatoes and plenty of steamed vegetables such as broccoli or thinly sliced savoy cabbage.

Serves: 4
Suitable for freezing

4 boneless, skinless chicken breasts
75g/2³⁄₄ oz reduced fat cream cheese
2 cloves garlic, crushed
2 tablespoons fresh herbs, chopped
eg parsley, thyme and chives
3 pieces fresh brown bread made into breadcrumbs
1 tablespoon fresh grated Parmesan
2 tablespoons plain flour
1 medium egg, beaten
salt and freshly ground black pepper

Preheat the oven to 200°C/400°F/gas mark 6
Make a horizontal slit in each chicken breast to form a pocket. In a small bowl mix together the cream cheese, garlic and herbs then season well. Divide the cream cheese mixture between each chicken pocket, press the edges of the chicken together to seal. Mix together the breadcrumbs and the Parmesan.

Roll the chicken breasts in flour, then egg, then the breadcrumb mixture. Place the coated chicken onto a non-stick baking sheet and chill for 30 minutes. Bake in the oven for 25-30 minutes or until golden and cooked through.

 Serve immediately.

It's easy to vary the chicken filling eg mix cream cheese with pesto or sun dried tomato paste and chopped olives for a Mediterranean flavour.

Per serving:

Energy: 333kcal   Protein: 49g   Carbohydrate: 15g   Fat: 9g

Seafood pasta

Served with salad, this low calorie recipe makes a complete meal.

Serves 4
Not suitable for freezing

350g/12oz dried spaghetti
350g/12oz broccoli florets
1 tablespoon oil
1 red chilli, finely chopped
2 cloves garlic, sliced
1 red pepper, sliced
4 tablespoons fish stock
450g/1lb uncooked shellfish eg mussels, clams
150g/5¹/₂oz shell-on prawns
4 tablespoons fresh parsley, chopped
salt and freshly ground black pepper

Cook the spaghetti in boiling water according to the pack instructions. Add the broccoli 5 minutes before the end of cooking time. Drain. Meanwhile, heat the oil in a non-stick pan and fry the chilli, garlic and pepper for 2-3 minutes.

Add the fish stock, shellfish and prawns, cover and simmer for 3-4 minutes or until the shellfish are cooked. Stir through the spaghetti, broccoli and parsley, season. Heat through and serve.

Shellfish contain cholesterol but blood cholesterol is more influenced by the amount of saturated fat in the diet and other factors such as being overweight.

Per serving:

Energy: 430kcal	Protein: 33.3g	Carbohydrate: 62g	Fat: 7.2g

Seafood pasta

Thai chicken with noodles

This recipe is a complete meal which combines lean meat, vegetables and noodles. It is low in calories and full of flavour.

Serves 4
Not suitable for freezing

1 teaspoon oil
2.5cm/1 inch fresh ginger, peeled and grated
1 clove garlic, crushed
2 boneless, skinless chicken breasts, sliced
1 red pepper, sliced
2 teaspoons red Thai curry paste
100g/3 ½oz mangetout
100g/3 ½oz baby sweetcorn, halved lengthways
300ml/ ½ pint chicken stock
50g/1 ¾oz creamed coconut,
made up to 300ml/ ½ pint with boiling water
200g/7oz thread egg noodles
1 bunch spring onions, sliced
grated rind and juice of 1 lime

Heat the oil in a large pan, add the ginger and garlic and fry for 1 minute. Add the chicken and red pepper and continue to fry for 3-4 minutes. Stir in the Thai curry paste, mangetout, sweetcorn, coconut mixture and the noodles. Bring to the boil. Cover and simmer for 5 minutes, or until the noodles are tender. Add the spring onions, lime rind and juice 1 minute before the end of cooking time. Serve immediately. If the mixture becomes a little dry whilst cooking add some extra chicken stock.

  Stir-frying uses a minimum amount of oil. As foods are cooked quickly, less of the vitamins are lost.

Per serving:

Energy: 371kcal	Protein: 29.4g	Carbohydrate: 40g	Fat: 11.4g

Sausage and bean hotpot

This one-pot meal should be served with some extra carbohydrate such as a jacket potato mashed without any butter or margarine - just a little semi-skimmed milk to keep fat down. For a vegetarian option, use vegetarian sausages or simply omit the sausages and using an extra can of beans.

Serves: 4
Not suitable for freezing

8 low fat sausages
I teaspoon oil
I onion, sliced
I clove garlic, crushed
I courgette, sliced
I x 400g can flageolet bean, drained and rinsed
I x 400g can cannelini beans, drained and rinsed
I x 500g jar passata (sieved tomatoes)
2 tablespoons wholegrain mustard
I tablespoon tomato purée

Grill the sausages under a preheated grill for 4-5 minutes until beginning to brown all over. Meanwhile, heat the oil in a non-stick saucepan and fry the onion, garlic and courgette for 3-4 minutes until softened. Stir in the remaining ingredients, including the sausages, stir well, cover and simmer for 20 minutes. Serve immediately.

Meat products like sausages tend to be high in fat. Choose the lower fat versions whenever possible.

Per serving:

Energy: 298kcal	Protein: 19.1g	Carbohydrate: 28g	Fat: 12.4g

Pork kebabs

A low calorie meat dish that should be served with carbohydrate, such as a mixture of wild and long grain rice and vegetables such as peas or sweetcorn. As this recipe is so low in fat, you could choose to combine it with a potato wedges, oven chips or garlic bread.

Serves: 4

Not suitable for freezing

350g/12oz extra lean pork steaks, cubed
24 ready-to-eat dried apricots
8 fresh sage leaves
2 small onions, cut into wedges
grated rind and juice of 1 large orange
1 tablespoon wholegrain mustard

Thread the pork, apricots, sage leaves and onion onto 8 skewers. Place in a large dish. Mix together the orange rind and juice and the mustard. Pour mixture over the kebabs. Leave to marinate in the fridge for at least 1 hour or preferably overnight. Place the kebabs under a preheated grill or on a barbecue and cook for 8-10 minutes, turning occasionally until browned and cooked through. Serve immediately.

 Using marinades which are not oil based gives food a delicious flavour without adding extra calories.

Per serving:

Energy: 166kcal	Protein: 20.8g	Carbohydrate: 13.8g	Fat: 3.5g

Pasta with spinach, blue cheese and crispy bacon

High fibre

Serve with mixed salad and chopped spring onions for a low calorie supper.
Serves: 4
Not suitable for freezing

350g/12oz dried pasta shapes
250g/8oz baby spinach leaves
50g/1³/₄oz dolcelatte cheese, cubed
12 cherry tomatoes, halved
3 slices, lean back bacon, grilled then chopped into pieces

Creative recipes for all occasions

Cook the pasta according to the pack instructions, drain then return to the pan. Stir through the remaining ingredients and toss until the spinach has wilted. Serve immediately.

 Pasta is a perfect starchy basis for meals for people with diabetes because of its low glycaemic index.

Per serving:

Energy: 384kcal	Protein: 16.4g	Carbohydrate: 68g	Fat: 7g

Parmesan risotto

The fat content of this recipe will vary depending on the added ingredients you use. Serve with an Italian style bread, such as ciabatta.

Serves 4
Not suitable for freezing

1.2 litres/2 pints boiling vegetable stock
a few strands of saffron
1 tablespoon olive oil
1 small onion, finely chopped
2 cloves garlic, crushed
350g/12oz risotto rice
125ml/4fl oz dry white wine
50g/1³/₄oz fresh Parmesan, grated
salt and freshly ground black pepper

Pour 4 tablespoons of the boiling stock into a small bowl, add the saffron and set aside.

Heat the oil in a large, heavy based frying pan. Add the onion and garlic and fry for 2-3 minutes. Add the rice and stir until coated in oil. Pour in wine, bring to the boil and simmer for 1-2 minutes, stirring.

Add a ladle full of stock. Simmer until all the liquid has been absorbed, stirring continuously. Continue this process until all the stock has been used, adding the saffron and the soaking liquid with the last addition of stock. Remove from the heat, stir in the Parmesan and season well.

Energy: 168kcal   Protein: 6.7g   Carbohydrate: 15.2g   Fat: 6.7g

Variations

Risotto is very versatile. You can vary the added ingredients according to what you have available. Why not try the following:

Tomato risotto

Before the final addition of the stock, stir in 12 halved cherry tomatoes, 2 tablespoons sun dried tomato paste, 4 sun-dried tomatoes sliced, and 1 tablespoon fresh chopped rosemary and then stir in the parmesan.

Mushroom risotto

Fry 450g (1 lb) mixed mushrooms in 2 tablespoons olive oil for 4-5 minutes or until cooked. Add the mushrooms and 1 tablespoon fresh, chopped thyme before the final addition of the stock. Before serving stir through 1 tablespoon grated Parmesan.

Olive oil is high in monounsaturated fat (which is a better choice) but is still as high in calories as other oils.

Easy
ENTERTAINING

Ricotta and red pepper pancakes with tomato sauce

Pancakes are traditional family favourites so try these wholemeal, savoury versions for something completely different.

Serves 4
Suitable for freezing

For the pancakes:
125g/4¹/₂oz wholemeal flour
1 egg, beaten
1 egg yolk
150ml/¹/₄ pint skimmed milk
150ml/¹/₄ pint water
1 tablespoon sesame seeds
1 tablespoon poppy seeds
15g/¹/₂ oz melted butter
a little oil for brushing pan

For the filling:
¹/₂ teaspoon oil
4 red peppers, deseeded and sliced
4 spring onions, sliced
1 clove garlic, crushed
1 x 250g carton ricotta cheese
4 tablespoons fresh parsley, chopped

For the tomato sauce:
2 x 150g cartons fresh tomato salsa
handful of basil, chopped

Creative recipes for all occasions

Make the pancakes by placing the flour, eggs, milk and water into a food processor or blender and blend until smooth. Stir in the sesame seeds, poppy seeds and the butter. Brush a small non-stick pan with a little oil then heat. Add 2 tablespoons of pancake mixture, spread over the pan and cook for 30 seconds on each side. Continue until all the mixture is used up (this should make approx 12 pancakes).

Heat the oil in a non-stick frying pan. Add the peppers, spring onions and garlic. Fry for 3-4 minutes until beginning to soften. Stir in the ricotta and parsley and heat through. Spoon a little of the ricotta mixture onto each pancake, roll up and keep warm. Heat the salsa and basil in a small pan and serve with the pancakes.

 When you fry always use the minimum amount of oil and a non-stick pan to try to keep the fat content down.

Per serving:

Energy: 215kcal	Protein: 10.6g	Carbohydrate: 22g	Fat: 11g

Mediterranean cod fillets

A low calorie fish dish but with little carbohydrate or fibre. Serve with pasta or new potatoes and a crisp green salad.
Serves 4
Not suitable for freezing

4 pieces of cod fillet, each
weighing approx 125g/4¹/₂ oz
50g/1³/₄ oz pitted black olives
2 anchovy fillets
4 sun-dried tomatoes, those stored in oil, drained
3 tablespoons fresh parsley, chopped
freshly ground black pepper

Pre-heat the oven to 200°C/400°F/gas mark 6
Place the cod fillets in a shallow, ovenproof dish. Put all the remaining ingredients into a blender or food processor and blend until combined but still retaining a little texture. Press the olive mixture onto the cod pieces, cover the dish with foil and bake for 10-12 minutes or until the fish is just cooked.
Serve immediately.

White fish is very low in fat and is an ideal protein source when you are trying to cut down on calories. Cook with no added fat to give a low calorie dish such as this.

Per serving:

| Energy: 155kcal | Protein: 242g | Carbohydrate: 0g | Fat: 6g |

Chicken with mushroom and tarragon sauce

Serve with brown rice or bulgar wheat and plenty of vegetables to increase the fibre and carbohydrate content of the meal.

Serves 4
Not suitable for freezing

600ml/1 pint good vegetable or chicken stock
1 onion, halved
1 cinnamon stick
4 boneless, skinless chicken breasts
1 teaspoon oil
250g/9oz button mushrooms, sliced
6 tablespoons light crème fraîche
2 tablespoons fresh tarragon, chopped
salt and freshly ground black pepper

Place the stock, onion and cinnamon stick in a medium saucepan. Bring to the boil. Add the chicken breasts, cover and simmer for 10-12 minutes or until the chicken is cooked through.

Heat the oil in a non-stick frying pan. Add the mushrooms and fry for 3-4 minutes. Add 4 tablespoons of the chicken cooking liquor to the frying pan and simmer for 1 minute. Add the chicken, crème fraîche and tarragon to the pan and heat through.

Poaching, like steaming, is a fat-free cooking method.

Per serving:

| Energy: 258kcal | Protein:41.1g | Carbohydrate: 3g | Fat:9.1g |

Pan fried trout with citrus and basil sauce

Serve this low calorie dish with a mixture of wild and long grain rice and steamed vegetables.

Serves 4

Not suitable for freezing

4 boneless, skinless trout fillets, weighing approx 100g/3¹/₂oz each

grated rind and juice of 2 oranges

3 tablespoons fresh basil, chopped

3 tablespoons light crème fraîche

salt and freshly ground black pepper

Place the trout fillets into a non-stick frying pan. Pour the orange rind and juice over the trout fillets. Cover and simmer gently for 5-6 minutes or until the fish is just cooked. Gently stir in the basil and crème fraîche and heat through. Season well and serve with new potatoes and plenty of vegetables or salad.

 To keep the fat down try not to add extra oil when cooking.

Per serving:

Energy: 154kcal	Protein: 20.2g	Carbohydrate: 3g	Fat: 6.9g

Crusted lamb steaks

Serve with low fat, high carbohydrate choices such as jacket or new potatoes and steamed vegetables. Remember vegetables and starchy foods should form the main part of a balanced meal.

Serves: 4

Not suitable for freezing

4 lean lamb steaks, each weighing approx 100g/3¹/₂oz

2 tablespoons pesto

4 tablespoons fresh granary breadcrumbs

salt and freshly ground black pepper

Preheat the oven to 200°C/400°F/gas mark 6.

Place the lamb steaks onto a baking tray. Mix together the pesto and bread-crumbs and use to top the lamb steaks. Place in the oven and cook for 15-20 minutes or until cooked to taste. Serve immediately.

Creative recipes for all occasions

Pan fried trout with citrus and basil sauce

You could use lean beef steaks for a change.

Per serving:

| Energy: 208kcal | Protein: 22g | Carbohydrate: 4g | Fat: 11g |

Chicken and prawn curry

High fibre

This recipe already contains vegetables so serve this dish with naan bread or popadoms, chutneys, chopped onion and raita. Take-away or ready prepared Indian or Chinese food can contain a lot more fat, salt and calories than a homemade version.

Serves 4
Not suitable for freezing

1 teaspoon oil
350g/12oz boneless, skinless chicken thighs, cubed
1 large onion, sliced
2 cloves garlic, crushed
2.5cm/1inch piece fresh ginger, finely chopped
1 cinnamom stick
6 cloves
6 cardamom pods, bruised
2 tablespoons medium curry paste
1 teaspoon ground turmeric
350g/12oz potatoes, cooked and cubed
100g/3½oz frozen peas
1 small cauliflower, cut into florets
1 x 400g can chopped tomatoes
300ml/½ pint vegetable stock
12 large cooked prawns

Heat the oil in a large saucepan. Add the chicken, onion, garlic and ginger and fry for 4-5 minutes. Add the spices and the curry paste to the pan and continue to cook for a further minute. Stir in the potatoes, peas, cauliflower, tomatoes and stock. Bring to the boil, cover and simmer for 10 minutes or until the cauliflower is tender adding the prawns 2 minutes before the end of cooking time.

 To bruise the cardamom pods, place on a chopping board and crush lightly with the back of a spoon - this will allow the flavours to be released.

Per serving:

| Energy: 337kcal | Protein: 35.5g | Carbohydrate: 24g | Fat: 11.6g |

Creative recipes for all occasions

Pan fried chicken livers with chickpea purée

Although pulses such as chickpeas contain carbohydrate you will still need to serve this dish with extra starchy foods to make a balanced meal.

Serves 2
Not suitable for freezing

I x 400g can chickpeas, drained and rinsed
I clove garlic, crushed
I sprig fresh thyme
450ml/³/₄ pint good chicken or vegetable stock
2 teaspoons oil
I red onion, cut into wedges
200g/7oz prepared chicken livers, halved
I tablespoon wholegrain mustard
6 tablespoons red wine or stock
2 tablespoons fresh parsley
4 tablespoons Greek yogurt

Place the chickpeas into a medium saucepan. Add the garlic, thyme and stock. Bring to the boil, cover and simmer for 15 minutes. Drain.

Meanwhile, heat the oil in a non-stick frying pan. Add the onions and fry over a low heat for 8-10 minutes until beginning to caramelise. Add the chicken livers and continue to cook for 2-3 minutes. Add the mustard and red wine and simmer for a further minute.

Purée the chickpeas until smooth, stir through the parsley and yogurt and season well. Serve the chicken livers with the chickpea purée. Pour over the pan juices and serve.

Liver is a rich source of iron and vitamins. Pregnant women are advised not to eat liver or liver products because of its high Vitamin A content. Large amounts of this vitamin can be harmful to the growing baby. Offal, like liver, is high in cholesterol but it is the saturated fat in food that is most harmful to blood cholesterol levels.

Per serving:

Energy: 194kcal	Protein: 15.9g	Carbohydrate: 13.9g	Fat: 6.9g

Fruity chicken

This dish is a poor source of carbohydrate - serve with couscous or rice and a selection of vegetables.

Serves 4

Not suitable for freezing

3 boneless, skinless chicken breasts, cubed
1 teaspoon Chinese five spice
150g/5¹/₂ oz pitted prunes
150g/5¹/₂ oz ready-to-eat dried apricots
1 cinnamon stick
1 tablespoon oil
1 onion, cut into wedges
1 teaspoon ground cinnamon
2 tablespoons blanched almonds, toasted

Rub the chicken with the Chinese five spice and set aside for 30 minutes. Meanwhile, place the prunes, apricots and cinnamon stick in a pan with 300ml/¹/₂ pint water and simmer for 20 minutes. Heat the oil in a non-stick frying pan. Add the onion and ground cinnamon and fry for 3-4 minutes. Add the chicken and brown on each side. Add the prune mixture, removing the cinnamon stick. Bring to the boil, cover and simmer for 15 minutes. Stir through the almonds and serve.

 Dried fruit can be used in sweet or savoury recipes as a great fibre provider.

Per serving:

Energy: 339kcal	Protein: 39.7g	Carbohydrate: 28g	Fat: 8.4g

Lamb with peas

Although this recipe includes potatoes, it should be served with extra carbohydrate such as bread, or with a starchy starter such as spicy bean paté and toast.

Serves 4

Not suitable for freezing

Creative recipes for all occasions

Fruity chicken

1.2 ltr/2 pints good lamb stock
450g/1lb new potatoes
12 shallots, peeled
2 large sprigs rosemary
250g/9oz frozen or fresh peas
1 teaspoon oil
4 lean lamb steaks each weighing approx 125g/4¹⁄₂oz
salt and freshly ground black pepper

Bring the lamb stock to the boil. Add the potatoes, shallots and rosemary to the pan. Simmer for 15-20 minutes or until the potatoes are tender, adding the peas 5 minutes before the end of cooking time. Remove the potatoes and peas from the cooking liquor and set aside, reserving the stock.

Heat the oil in a large non-stick frying pan. Add the lamb and cook for 3-4 minutes on each side or until cooked to your liking. Add 150ml/¹⁄₄ pint of the reserved stock to the frying pan and reduce slightly. Add the cooked vegetables, heat through and serve.

 Frozen or tinned vegtables are useful alternatives if you do not have any fresh.

Per serving:

Energy: 332kcal	Protein: 31.6g	Carbohydrate: 26.1g	Fat: 11.9g

Lamb fillet with ratatouille and rosti

This is an ideal recipe for entertaining. Serve with a higher carbohydrate starter such as spicy bean pâté and toast as this dish is a poor source of carbohydrate.
Serves 4
Rosti suitable for freezing

450g/1lb lean lamb fillet, sliced into 2.5cm/1inch thick pieces
2 cloves garlic, crushed
1 large sprig rosemary
1 tablespoon olive oil
1 onion, sliced
2 courgettes, sliced
1 small aubergine, quartered and chopped

Creative recipes for all occasions

1 x 400g can chopped tomatoes
1 x 400g can chopped tomatoes
1 red pepper
1 sprig fresh thyme

For the rosti:
450g/1lb potatoes
1 tablespoon flour
1 medium egg
salt and freshly ground black pepper

Place the lamb, 1 clove garlic, rosemary and 1 teaspoon of olive oil into a bowl, stir and leave to marinate for at least 30 minutes.

Heat 1 teaspoon of oil in a medium non-stick pan add the remaining clove of garlic, onion, courgette and aubergine and fry for 4-5 minutes until beginning to soften. Add the tomatoes, pepper and thyme, cover and simmer for 30 minutes. Remove the lid and continue to cook for 10 minutes, until most of the liquid has evaporated.

Meanwhile, boil the potatoes for 5 minutes. Drain. Grate coarsely when cool enough to handle. Mix together with the flour and egg, season well then shape into 8 patties.

Heat the remaining oil in the frying pan. Add the rosti and fry over a medium heat for 4-5 minutes on each side until golden and cooked through. Remove from the heat and keep warm. Add the lamb to the pan and fry for 2-3 minutes on each side, until cooked to your liking. Serve with the rosti and the ratatouille.

 Always choose lean meat to reduce the fat content of recipes.

Per serving:

Energy: 418kcal	Protein: 29.2g	Carbohydrate: 30g	Fat: 20g

Pork stroganoff

A rich meat sauce with little carbohydrate or vegetable within the recipe. Serve with tagliatelle or rice and steamed vegetables such as green beans and broccoli.
Serves 4
Not suitable for freezing

I tablespoon oil	
450g/1lb pork tenderloin, (or lean pork steaks) sliced	
I onion, sliced	
I clove garlic, crushed	
2 sprigs fresh thyme	
250g/9oz mushrooms, sliced	
I tablespoon Dijon mustard	
I teaspoon paprika	
6 tablespoons Greek yogurt	
6 tablespoons light crème fraîche	

Heat the oil in a non-stick frying pan. Add the pork, onion, garlic and thyme. Fry for 3-4 minutes or until the pork begins to brown. Add the mushrooms and continue to cook for 3-4 minutes. Stir through the remaining ingredients and heat through gently, without allowing to boil. Serve immediately.

 Pork stroganoff traditionally uses high fat ingredients like soured cream. This recipe loses none of its flavour by using lower fat alternatives.

Per serving:

Energy: 237kcal	Protein: 28.7g	Carbohydrate: 3.4g	Fat: 12.2g

Coriander and lime pork ✓   low fat

For a low calorie main meal serve with rice or new potatoes and steamed vegetables such as leeks or carrots.

Serves 4

Not suitable for freezing

4 lean pork steaks each weighing approx 100g/3½oz
grated rind and juice of 2 limes
4 tablespoons fresh coriander, chopped
2 cloves garlic, crushed
2 tablespoons dry white wine or vegetable stock
I tablespoon olive oil
2 teaspoons runny honey
salt and freshly ground black pepper

Creative recipes for all occasions

Place the pork steaks into a shallow, non-metallic dish. In a separate bowl mix the remaining ingredients together. Pour over the pork steaks. Season well and leave to marinade for at least 2 hours.

Pre-heat the grill to high. Place the pork steaks on a foil lined baking sheet and grill for 8-10 minutes until cooked through, turning half way through cooking time and basting with the marinade. Serve immediately.

 Although honey is high in sugar it can be included in cooking to add flavour without adding significant calories or harming blood glucose control.

Per serving:

Energy: 209kcal	Protein:34.3g	Carbohydrate: 3.2g	Fat: 5g

Polenta with pan fried maple pork

Polenta is a starchy carbohydrate food made from maize that is a staple in Northern Italy. This makes a delicious Italian style meal when served with grilled tomatoes and green beans.
Serves 6
Not suitable for freezing

For the maple pork
I tablespoon Dijon mustard
3 tablespoon maple syrup
I tablespoon fresh sage, chopped
4 lean loin pork chops
salt and freshly ground black pepper

For the polenta
2ltrs/3¹/₂ pints water
325g/11¹/₂oz quick cook polenta
2 tablespoons fresh Parmesan, grated
2 tablespoons fresh parsley, chopped

Blend together the mustard, maple syrup and sage in shallow dish. Add the pork to the dish and coat with the sauce. Leave to marinate for at least 30 minutes. Heat the grill to high. Place the chops onto a foil lined grill pan and grill for 8-10 minutes, turning occasionally until cooked through. Meanwhile make the polenta. Bring the water to the boil then add the polenta in a steady stream stirring continuously. Cook over a low heat for 5 minutes stirring continuously until thickened. Stir in the Parmesan and parsley and season well, pour onto a baking tray and leave to set. Cut into wedges, then grill for 2-3 minutes on each side until beginning to brown, then serve.

Serve polenta with other meals as a change from bread and potatoes.

Per serving:

Energy: 400kcal	Protein: 33.7g	Carbohydrate: 45g	Fat: 9g

Braised beef with beans and olives

High fibre

A higher calorie dish best served with low fat carbohydrate such as potato mashed with a little skimmed milk and steamed vegetables such as spinach or cabbage.
Serves 4
Suitable for freezing

I tablespoon oil
450g/1lb lean stewing steak, cubed
I onion, sliced
I clove garlic, crushed
I tablespoon plain flour
150ml/¼ pint red wine
300ml/½ pint stock
3 tablespoons tomato purée
2 x 400g cans mixed beans, drained and rinsed
100g/3½ oz pitted black or green olives

Pre-heat the oven to 180°C/350°F/gas mark 4.
Heat the oil in a flameproof casserole dish. Add the steak, onion and garlic and fry for 3-4 minutes or until the meat is browned then stir through the flour. Add the wine, stock and tomato purée and stir. Cover tightly then place in the oven and cook for 1½- 2 hours or until the meat is tender. Stir in the beans and olives, return to the oven for 10 minutes then serve.

Use less meat by adding beans to casseroles and other meat dishes. This reduces the fat content and beans are a cheaper source of protein.

Per serving:

Energy: 402kcal	Protein: 39g	Carbohydrate: 34g	Fat: 10.5g

Creative recipes for all occasions

Sauces, marinades and dressings

Bring meat, fish or vegetables to life by serving with a delicious sauce (salsa) or marinating before cooking. Shop bought dressings can be higher in fat. Try some of these ideas to add interest to your meals.

Sauces

Fresh herb aioli

Simply blend together 1 small green chilli, 4 tablespoons of fat-free mayonnaise, 4 tablespoons light crème fraîche and 4 tablespoons fresh herbs such as coriander, parsley and dill. Season well and serve.

Fruity salsa

Mix together 1 finely chopped red onion, 350g/12oz quartered cherry tomatoes, 1/4 finely chopped cucumber, 1 mango peeled and chopped, grated rind and juice of 1 lime.

Marinades

Spicy/Tandoori

Mix together 3 tablespoons tandoori paste, 1 clove crushed garlic, 2 tablespoons natural yogurt and 1 tablespoon lemon juice. Use to marinate 2 boneless, skinless chicken breasts or tofu for a vegetarian option.

Oriental

Mix together 1 clove crushed garlic, 1 tablespoon grated fresh ginger, 1 tablespoon soy sauce, 3 tablespoons stock and 1 tablespoon chilli sauce. Use to marinate enough meat or vegetables for two people. Thicken the marinade with 1/2 teaspoon cornflour and pour over the cooked meat or vegetables.

 If you have marinated raw meat, the marinade must be heated to boiling point for at least 2 minutes if serving as an accompaniment.

Dressings

Apple and mustard dressing

Mix together 8 tablespoons of apple juice, 1 tablespoon wholegrain mustard, 2 tablespoons white wine vinegar and 2 teaspoons runny honey.

Italian dressing

Mix together 2 tablespoons pesto, 1 tablespoon white wine vinegar and 2 tablespoons of olive oil.

Grilled fruit and nut loaf with plums and blackberries

A delicious dessert when entertaining. It's not too rich or over-indulgent.
Serves 4
Not suitable for freezing

15g/¹/₂ oz butter
8 plums, halved and stoned
125g/4¹/₂ oz blackberries
2 tablespoons caster sugar
4 slices fruit and nut loaf, toasted

Melt the butter in a non-stick frying pan. Add the plums and fry over a gentle heat until slightly softened. Stir through the blackberries and sugar and cook for 1-2 minutes until the sugar has dissolved. Serve the fruit on the toasted fruit and nut loaf.

 Although it is preferable to use unsaturated fats rather than saturated animal fats, you can use small amounts of butter where it contributes flavour.

Per serving:

Energy: 184kcal	Protein: 3g	Carbohydrate: 32g	Fat: 6g

Grilled fruit and nut loaf
with plums and blackberries

Chestnut and chocolate cream layers

This chocolate dessert is both easy and delicious without being loaded with fat and calories. It's great for entertaining.

Serves 4

Not suitable for freezing

6 tablespoons chestnut purée
2 tablespoons cocoa powder
40g/1½oz soft dark brown sugar
1 x 150g carton low fat natural yogurt
1 x 200g carton light crème fraîche
1 large orange peeled and cut into small chunks
grated plain chocolate to decorate

Mix together the chestnut purée, cocoa and sugar then stir in half of the crème fraîche. Beat together the yogurt and remaining crème fraîche. Place a few pieces of orange in the base of 4 serving glasses. Spoon over a little yogurt mixture then top with some of the chestnut mixture. Continue to layer until all the ingredients are used up. To serve: top with a little grated chocolate.

 Chestnuts are lower in fat than other nuts and make a delicious ingredient for puddings.

Per serving:

Energy: 148kcal	Protein: 4.3g	Carbohydrate: 18.7g	Fat: 6.8g

Summer berry charlotte

Ideal for midweek or Sunday lunch. Serve with vanilla ice cream.

Serves 6

Not suitable for freezing

1 x 450g pack frozen mixed berries, defrosted
25g/1oz butter
40g/1½oz soft light brown sugar
40g/1½oz no-added sugar muesli
125g/4½oz granary bread, made into coarse breadcrumbs

Creative recipes for all occasions

Pre-heat the oven to 200°C/400°F/gas mark 6.
Place the berries and any juice into a shallow ovenproof dish. Melt the butter in a frying pan then add the sugar, muesli and breadcrumbs. Sprinkle over the fruit then cook for 20 minutes or until golden and bubbling.

Use this delicious topping for other fruits such as tinned pears and blackberries.

Per serving:

Energy: 255kcal	Protein: 7.3g	Carbohydrate: 47.7g	Fat: 5.5g

Chocolate and orange soufflé

Low fat

Cocoa powder gives this dessert a lovely chocolatey taste.
Serves 6
Not suitable for freezing

a little vegetable oil for greasing
grated rind and juice of 2 large oranges
75g/2³/₄oz caster sugar
4 large egg whites, beaten until stiff
25g/1oz cocoa powder
2 tablespoons orange liqueur
4 tablespoons light crème fraîche

Pre-heat the oven to 200°C/400°F/gas mark 6.
Lightly grease 6 dariole moulds or teacups. In a small pan, heat the orange rind, juice and caster sugar for 3-4 minutes until syrupy. Pour the syrup over the egg whites and beat for 2 minutes. Fold in the cocoa and liqueur then pour into the moulds. Cook in the oven for 5-6 minutes or until risen. Serve topped with the crème fraîche.

Traditional chocolate soufflé has all the added fat and calories that comes with using chocolate.

Per serving:

Energy: 87kcal	Protein: 3g	Carbohydrate: 16g	Fat: 1.6g

Poached spiced pears

An ideal low calorie dessert that is special enough for entertaining.

Serves 4
Not suitable for freezing

200ml (7fl oz) red wine
3 tablespoons lemon juice
50g/1³/₄oz caster sugar
1 cinnamon stick
3 cardamom pods
1 teaspoon vanilla essence
4 ripe pears, peeled and halved

Put the wine, lemon juice, sugar, cinnamon stick, cardamom pods and vanilla essence into a large pan with 300ml/¹/₂ pint water. Heat gently until the sugar has dissolved. Add the pears. Cover and simmer gently for 10-12 minutes or until the pears are softened slightly. Serve the pears with a little of the cooking liquid. Serve hot or chilled with a little light crème fraîche.

Fruit makes an ideal basis for puddings.

Per serving:

Energy: 147kcal	Protein: 0g	Carbohydrate: 30g	Fat: 0g

Peach clafoutis

A pudding to impress the family or to use when entertaining. Serve after a main course which is low in fat.

Serves 6
Not suitable for freezing

4 medium eggs, beaten
100g/3¹/₂oz caster sugar
50g/1³/₄oz plain flour
250ml/8 fl oz skimmed milk
25g/1oz butter
750g/1¹/₂ lb fresh peaches, stoned and quartered

Pre-heat the oven to 200°C/400°F/gas mark 6.
In a large bowl beat together the eggs and sugar. Whisk in the flour until smooth then whisk in the milk. Melt the butter and stir into the batter.

Place the peaches into a 8 x 18 cm/11 x 7 inch shallow ovenproof dish. Pour over the batter then bake for 35-40 minutes until golden and the batter is just set. Serve immediately.

For some pudding recipes you cannot replace the sugar with sweetener and get the same results. Use sugar when baking or for aerating mixtures.

Per serving:

Energy: 222kcal	Protein: 7g	Carbohydrate: 32g	Fat: 8g

Fruit Fool

Low fat

A low calorie pudding which the whole family will enjoy.
Serves 6
Not suitable for freezing

1 x 410g can light evaporated milk,
chilled in the tin for at least two hours

450g/1lb summer berries such as strawberries,
raspberries, blackberries, defrosted if frozen

2 tablespoons icing sugar

Pour the evaporated milk into a large bowl and whisk until thickened and doubled in volume. Purée the fruits, reserving a few for decoration, push through a sieve to remove any seeds. Stir the purée and the icing sugar into the whisked evaporated milk then spoon into 6 serving dishes. Top with reserved fruit and serve.

Evaporated milk is lower in fat than cream and can be whipped and used in its place if chilled thoroughly.

Per serving:

Energy: 103kcal	Protein: 7.3g	Carbohydrate: 12.4g	Fat: 2.9g

Jellied berry terrine

This is a low calorie dessert and a delicious alternative to fruit salad.
Serve with a little Greek yogurt or crème fraîche.
Serves 6

6 slices thin white sliced bread, crusts removed
2 sachets blackcurrant, raspberry
or strawberry sugar-free jelly
450g/1lb prepared fresh berries such
as strawberries, raspberries, blueberries

Line a 900g/2lb loaf tin with clingfilm. Line the prepared tin with pieces of bread to cover completely. Dissolve the jelly in 300ml/½ pint boiling water then make up to 900ml/1½ pints with cold water. Arrange the fruit in the tin then cover with the remaining bread. Pour over the jelly, cover with clingfilm then place in the fridge to set. Turn out onto a serving platter and remove the clingfilm.

 Sugar-free jelly is virtually free from fat and calories too.

Per serving:

| Energy: 105kcal | Protein: 3.6g | Carbohydrate: 22g | Fat: 0g |

Tropical frozen yogurt

This low fat frozen yogurt can be made with any variety of fruits and is delicious served with a selection of fresh tropical fruits such as kiwi, mango and pineapple.
Serves 6

1 x 142g can pineapple in natural juice, drained
1 mango, peeled, stoned and chopped
flesh of 2 passion fruits
600ml/1 pint low fat natural yogurt
2 tablespoons icing sugar

Place the pineapple and mango into a blender or food processor and blend until smooth. Stir through the remaining ingredients then transfer to a freezerproof container. Freeze for at least 8 hours or until solid.

Creative recipes for all occasions

Jellied berry terrine

Low fat frozen yogurt makes a delicious alternative to ice-cream.

Per serving:

Energy: 97kcal	Protein: 6g	Carbohydrate: 18g	Fat: 1g

Vanilla ice cream

low fat

Although you can use any sort of ice cream here are some home-made recipes to impress your family and friends.
Serves 6

2 x 425g cans low fat ready made custard
1 x 200g carton light crème fraîche
1 teaspoon vanilla essence

Mix together all the ingredients and transfer to a rigid freezerproof container. Freeze for about 2 hours, then beat with a fork. Return to the freezer and freeze until firm.

Per serving:

Energy: 168kcal	Protein: 7g	Carbohydrate: 26g	Fat: 5g

Variations
Lemon meringue ice cream
Follow the basic vanilla ice cream recipe. Having frozen the ice-cream for two hours, stir through 3 tablespoons lemon curd and 50g/1³/₄ oz lightly crushed meringue, then continue to freeze until solid.

Raspberry ripple ice cream
Follow the basic vanilla ice cream recipe. Halfway through the freezing time lightly fold through 200g/7oz puréed raspberries.

Although ice cream can be high in fat and sugar it is fine to eat it in small amounts as part of a balanced diet.

Creative recipes for all occasions

Lemon and banana brulée

low fat

This tasty low calorie dessert is virtually fat free.
Serves 4
Not suitable for freezing

1 banana, sliced
1 x 250g tub Quark
2 tablespoons lemon curd
4 teaspoons demerara sugar

Preheat the grill to high.
Divide the banana between 4 ramekin dishes. Mix together the Quark and the lemon curd. Spoon into the ramekins and smooth out. Sprinkle over the sugar, then place the ramekins under the grill for 1 minute or until the sugar has caramelised. Chill for 30 minutes or until the caramel has set. Serve immediately.

 As Quark is fat free it can be used instead of cream cheese in recipes.

Per serving:

Energy: 111kcal	Protein: 10g	Carbohydrate: 18g	Fat: 0.4g

Index

Creative recipes for all occasions

Easy entertaining

Delicious desserts

Index 2

Special requirements

If you are following a vegetarian, gluten-free or milk-free diet this index will help you to see at a glance which recipes you can use. **However, you must still check the food label to ensure that the particular ingredients you choose are in line with any special requirements you may have.**

Other recipes included in the book can be adapted but may require the use of special ingredients and changes to the method described.

Creative recipes for all occasions

Creative recipes for all occasions

Further information

The BDA *Careline* offers help and support on all aspects of diabetes. We provide a confidential service which takes general enquires from people with diabetes, their carers and from healthcare professionals. Our trained staff can give you the latest information on topics such as care of your diabetes, blood glucose levels, diet, illness, pregnancy, insurance, driving, welfare benefits and employment.

If you would like further information on any aspect of diabetes telephone or write to the British Diabetic Association *Careline*

10 Queen Anne Street
London
W1M 0BD

Tel: 0171 636 6112
Minicom: 0171 462 2757
email: careline@diabetes.org.uk

The BDA Catalogue describes our full range of books and leaflets. For copies of this and other BDA leaflets, please write to:
BDA Distribution Department
PO Box 1
Portishead
Bristol BS20 8DJ
Tel: 0800 585088

BDA Head Office: 10 Queen Anne Street, London W1M 0BD. Tel 0171 323 1531
BDA Scotland: 34 West George St, Glasgow G2 1DA. Tel 0141 332 2700
BDA North West: 65 Bewsey St, Warrington WA2 7JQ. Tel 01925 653281
BDA West Midlands: 1 Eldon Court, Eldon St, Walsall WS1 2JP. Tel 01922 614500
BDA Northern Ireland: 257 Lisburn Road, Belfast, BT9 7EN. Tel 01232 666646
BDA Wales: Plas Gwynt, Sophia Close, Cardiff CF1 9TD. Tel 01222 668276

A charity helping people with diabetes and supporting diabetes research
Registered Charity No. 215199

Creative recipes for all occasions